INTO THE MOON
HEART, MIND, BODY, SOUL

INTO THE MOON

HEART, MIND, BODY, SOUL

THE NATIVE WOMEN'S WRITING CIRCLE

EDITED BY
LENORE KEESHIG-TOBIAS

Sister Vision
Black Women and Women of Colour Press

96 97 98 99 ML 5 4 3 2 1

Canadian Cataloguing in Publication Data
Main entry under title:
Into the Moon
Heart, Mind, Body, Soul

ISBN 1-896705-04-9

1. Canadian literature (English) - Indian authors.*
2. Canadian literature (English) - Women authors.*
3. Canadian literature (English) - 20th century.*
4. Indian women - Canadian - Literary collections.
   1.Keeshig-Tobias, Lenore.

PS 8235.16157 1996   C810.8'09287   C96-930072-7

Editor: Lenore Keeshig-Tobias
Cover art & Illustrations: Darla Fisher-Odjig
Book design & layout: ART WORK

Represented in Canada by the Literary Press Group
Distributed in Canada by General Distribution
Represented and distributed in the U.S.A. by InBook (Division of
LPC Group)
Represented in Britain by Turnaround Ltd

Printed in Canada by union labour

SISTER VISION
Black Women and Women of Colour Press
P.O. Box 217, Station E
Toronto, Ontario
Canada M6H 4E2
(416) 595-5033

Into the Moon: Heart, Mind, Body, Soul, would not have been possible without the dedication and commitment of the Association for Native Development in the Performing and Visual Arts and Sister Vision Press, Chee Meegwetch

I have a personal belief that when women of all nations/colours pass from this world to the spirit world part of their spirit goes into the moon. When we with our different beliefs sit under our Grandmother for guidance, love, affirmation, it is all within the spirit of our Grandmother's gifts. Young and old, we all give to our Grandmother. When we write, we give of ourselves to women. Maybe some will see themselves in our stories or be touched in some way, maybe not. But for me it is a passing, a giving.

Cat Cayuga

Who will I have when you leave me here? I am afraid.

You will have your Moon to keep you company, inside and above you.

Barbara LaValley

CONTENTS

OPENING PRAYER   *Jacqui Lavalley*

INTRODUCTION   *Beth Brant*   **1**

WHO WE ARE   **3**

Lee Johns   *Lee Johns*   **5**

A Long Road   *Carol Loft*   **6**

The Yellow Girl   *Banakonda K.K. Bell*   **9**

Between Worlds   *Monica McKay*   **11**

Gwe Whi   *Dawn Ireland-Noganosh*   **14**

I am Seneca   *Barbara LaValley*   **15**

A Native Woman   *Jane Peloquin*   **17**

I Am   *Cat Cayuga*   **18**

WHAT WE DO   **19**

An Average Day   *Banakonda K.K. Bell*   **21**

Program Assistant   *Monica McKay*   **23**

Average Workday   *Dawn Ireland-Noganosh*   **24**

Cashier   *June Cayuga*   **25**

No Flowers, Please   *Barbara LaValley*   **26**

I Write   *Cat Cayuga*   **28**

WHAT WE SEE   29

line by line

I   *Joy/JANE/barbara/Joy*   *31*

II   *Jane/BARBARA/joy/Jane*   *32*

III   *Barbara/joy/JANE/Barbara*   *33*

IV   *Jane/BARBARA/joy/Jane*   *34*

V   *Barbara/Joy/jane/Barbara*   *36*

theme writing

Mother Earth   *Carol Loft*   *37*

Earth Day   *Monica McKay*   *38*

Of Earth and Sky   *Barbara LaValley*   *40*

Poem   *Cat Cayuga*   *43*

Poem   *June Cayuga*   *44*

Without Beauty   *Monica McKay*   *45*

The Calling   *Lee Johns*   *46*

visual imagery

Clear the Way for Technology   *Lee Johns*   **48**

Variation I   *Lee Johns*   **49**

This Picture of Trees   *Banakonda K.K. Bell*   **51**

Clearcut   *Monica McKay*   **52**

Trees   *Barbara LaValley*   **54**

Man-made Disease   *Dawn Ireland-Noganosh*   **55**

Standing   *Cat Cayuga*   **56**

There Has to be Balance   *June Cayuga*   **57**

beginnings and endings

Mother's Pride   *Dawn Ireland-Noganosh*   **58**

Survivor   *Carol Loft*   **60**

The Walk   *Monica McKay*   **62**

Winged Shadows   *Barbara LaValley*   **63**

Where You Fly I Fly   *Cat Cayuga*   **64**

A Lesson from Nature   *June Cayuga*   **65**

WRITE SPACES 67

> The Place I Write   *Dawn Ireland-Noganosh*   *69*

> Out of Chaos   *Carol Loft*   *71*

> My Workspace   *Monica McKay*   *72*

> My Workspace/Where I Write
> *Barbara LaValley*   *73*

STRENGTH 75

> Into the Moon   *Barbara LaValley*   *77*

> Giigs   *Monica McKay*   *79*

> Of Be(long)ing   *Barbara LaValley*   *81*

> From Loneliness   *Cat Cayuga*   *82*

STORIES TO TELL 83

> Dance Til You Wake   *Jane Peloquin*   *85*

> That Cousin   *Cat Cayuga*   *87*

> Discovery   *Barbara LaValley*   *89*

> Turtledream   *Cat Cayuga*   *91*

> Monologue   *Jane Peloquin*   *97*

> Final Chapter   *Barbara LaValley*   *101*

CLOSING PRAYER   *Jacqui Lavalley*   *109*

THE WOMEN   110

OPENING PRAYER

NOKOMIS SONG

Wai yaa hai
G'chi Ogima Kwe
Wai yaa hai
G'chi Ogima Kwe
Wai yaa hai
G'chi Ogima Kwe
Chi chii baa kae
G'chi Ogima

Wai yaa hai
Big Chief Woman
Wai yaa hai
Big Chief Woman
Wai yaa hai
Big Chief Woman
She's really cooking
Big Chief Woman

Indigenous Women of the Americas

Boozho! Nimoshehn nozhe. Miingan Kwe n'dishnekaz.

From time to time, a question arises in my mind: "How can we heal as a people?"

We cannot move forward and be strong unless we turn ourselves around as a people. This means looking, learning, and recognizing the subjugation, humiliation and painful experiences we share as Indigenous women, children and men. Through this exchange we can all begin that special kind of healing.

Jacqui Lavalley

Introduction

Beth Brant

CAT CAYUGA TELLS US, "I WRITE BY SPONTANEOUS COMBUSTION". I often think that this is the way with us — First Nations women who pick up pen and paper, who tap out letters on type-writers or computers. The stories are burning inside us, heating the blood, firing our activism, sparking the dialogues between us and others. Story emerges in whatever form it needs to take — poetry, fiction, creative documentary — and ignites the very spaces surrounding us.

When asked to facilitate a writing workshop for Native women in Toronto, I entered the process with joy and honour. Working together, we could name the entities that often circumscribe our lives: those entities that have been called self-hate or self-doubt, that spring from the internalization of colonial rule. None of us has been spared this internal struggle. Yet we have survived it. This book is another testament to that survival, that resistance.

During those intense two days of workshop, we learned that we are not alone. While this may seem like a cliché or an oversimplification of our varied battles with the structures and institutions that seek to destroy us, the realization that First

Nations women constitute *community* is an epiphany for many of us — a spiritual event that can change our lives. Sharing our stories with each other, putting those stories on paper, recognizing the truth between us, guiding each other — this is the stuff of the natural order of community. Choosing to share this epiphany with those who are outside our circle is an act of generosity and faith.

We laughed together, we cried together, we ate donuts and drank coffee together, we wrote together, we made magic together. The writing-spirits were hovering and warming us with their presence. What emerged from those two days was an act of spontaneous combustion — truth and love. Such simple things really, but taking on greater proportions as we hurl the words into the places that have sought to confine us or define us, into the spaces bereft of our culture, into the cosmos of a new beginning for our Nations.

The women in this book are warriors, carriers of truth; flesh, blood, bone, hair; born from the old ways, rebirthing themselves through the power of words, without ever losing touch with the old, the traditional, the natural. You, the reader, are witness to the fire of creation.

WHO WE ARE

Lee Johns

Lee Johns

I AM, ALWAYS WAS, AND ALWAYS WILL BE OJIBWA, POTTAWATTOMI. Anishinabe Kwe. My name is Lee Johns. My Anishnabe name means Chief Thunderbird Woman and was given to me through a traditional ceremony at my home, Neyaashiinigmiing. My clan is Loon Clan. For five years now, I have been carrying this identity with me. It has helped me deeply. It has centred me.

I come from a large family of nine children — I have five sisters and three brothers. I am the fourth oldest.

My father passed away to the spirit world seven years ago.

My mother lives at home on the reserve, trying desperately to teach her children to live on their own, reminding them that she isn't going to be around forever.

She teaches me so much, reflecting through herself the Earth Mother. I see the Earth in her when I think of her and see her work. I love her.

I grew up on the reserve and attended the Catholic school there, learning about Jesus and God, but always feeling that there was a greater understanding. There was a truth that needed to be found where I as Anishinabe was concerned.

It's so hard to talk about myself right now. So much healing is taking place from the physical abuse, emotional abuse and spiritual abuse. There is so much confusion in trying to see what is mine and what isn't. A lot of bad things are just blanked out, not wanting to be remembered.

I have a daughter; she is beautiful, a real gift. She has helped me balance my life as a woman, to look for something better, for her and for me.

A Long Road

Carol Loft

Many of us
Mohawk mother — White father
Mother the strong link — father in the background
Socially isolated, extremely shy and backwards
Too sensitive, carrying much pain
Confused and searching,

First to the external world, than internally

Grandmother strong force in my young life,
        Not always positive — much more negative
Married young, to get away to a
        better life, away from so much
        nothing, away from poverty
More confused, frightened and not sure what
        I'm to do
Always fighting, never wanting to be owned, or
        told what to do

Deep, deep down I knew there was
        a me, but why did it take so long to emerge?

A mother now, of a baby boy, who's so
        beautiful, but I refuse to be his
Mother — why — too young, irresponsible,
        scared, no parenting skills
Passed back and forth the first year of his
        life between his grandmothers, until I
        finally took him home
Over the years always unhappy, never "truly"
        happy — what is fun?

Again a mother — this time a baby girl whom
    I kept at home
    I loved her, but she still got the
Unloving me, many, many times

My husband stuck by, through thick and thin
    I often question why
As years went by I mellowed out more
    and more — but always that feeling of
    not quite accomplished
      of emptiness
        of fear and anger
          of so much unhappiness
A third child, our "special" baby — we're not
    her birth parents, but we're her
    Real parents — a beautiful, loving child
      — so lucky, we are

Went back to school, to upgrade and get
    my grade 12
    What a shock — I had to face the
    real world

I can't believe the pain that people inflict
    on others
I continued my education into college,
    again I had to take the blinders
      off — WHAT PAIN AND MISERY THE WORLD
      CONTAINS!

Now I work part-time, looking forward to
      a full-time job
      I feel so old, so wise, so
      confused,
      BUT MORE AT PEACE WITH MYSELF

I still have a long road to travel down
      to discover why I feel the way I do
        do
          — in the meantime I come to
          workshops like these to become
            more aware
                — to understand
                — to stay sane!

The Yellow Girl

Banakonda K. K. Bell

ONCE THERE WAS THIS YELLOW GIRL BORN ON THE FLOOR OF A CAB, on the way out of a reserve. She was four pounds. She grew up mostly alone, as a child among grown-ups. There were other children but somehow she was from the beginning an outsider, or, more aptly, a one-foot-inner, one-foot-outer.

All around her knives flashed, beer bottles were broken, boots and fists hit flesh. Blood was spilled. Women cowered in the aftermath, resigned. Men lost their pain in unconsciousness.

But in the night, in between the bouts of spilling and breaking each other, my Grandmother would sit with us in the kitchen by the wood-stove, with her tin cup of tea, rocking, telling us stories, rocking us with her words, her memories.

It was her refuge, and the conception of seedling dreams, that kept her going, past the loss, the separation, the strange home and ways that the non-Native intervention brought her.

She took her Grandmother's intervention stories to the bush, the rivers and to her dreams and wove them anew and separated herself almost completely from the physical world of humans, hiding, escaping in the natural world around her.

She even fancied that she had special relationships with trees and birds and plants. She made herself special in that world because she didn't count in the other.

And then one day she was taken away from it all. While in school, skipping, she heard the voice of her mother, calling. And she ran to this half-stranger.

She met her new sister, three weeks old. And then, with her father, mother and sister, she hitch-hiked to the city.

Subways, escalators and cockroaches, a one-room home at Gerrard and Parliament, and no bush, no rivers, no place to hide.

In the schoolyard, kids teased her because she talked "stupid," comparing things to trees and rivers and sky.

Once she brought a white cockroach to school in a jar — thinking that she was doing something wonderful. She was met with disgust and horror.

She felt shame but didn't know why.

When summer came, she would lie on the veranda and look up at the trees and pretend she was back home in the bush. Family Services sent her to a "fresh air camp." A counsellor took to her, reached out to her — walked into her isolation. It was there that she began to dream again, to transport her experience into the city, into a personal identity and pursuit.

She would work with people, her people. She'd stick it out in school and learn.

And she did, for awhile, tenuously playing her marginal role, struggling for membership while ambivalent as to whether she really wanted it.

She left school at 13 after finishing a two-year commercial course. She got work in a travel agency by lying about her age, and she left home. Two years later, she went to work with emotionally disturbed children at Browndale. There she met a man, a journalist.

A year later she married, stayed in university for four years, had a baby girl the last year and did not accept her scholarship to Osgoode Hall.

I was an enchanted mother for three years and then worked at the Metis and Non-Status Association as Assistant Director, Ahbenoojery — that grew out of that. Children's Aid from there, and another baby girl. Pedahbun Lodge from there. And here I am on the other side of two relationships with another girl child and now another birth but this time...

Between Worlds

Monica McKay

I'M SITTING HERE FEELING LIKE I'M BEING PULLED INTO THE EARTH. It's not a frightening feeling at all. It feels big, and I'm frustrated with that, because I sense this is important — not only for me, but for everyone in this room. I wish I could write as quickly as the thoughts and feelings that rush through me.

My main thought, as I listened to the other women, was "I wish I had said that." I realized in those moments that I was protecting myself — when I talk about my life, describing who I am and what is important in my life.

I have a sense of my soul and spirit undressing. So when the stories and words quit coming from within, I feel naked.

My work involves bringing Native and non-Native people together to look at our relationship and to tell our stories. I've realized that this is my path, and the teachers I seek — spiritual, traditional and from other cultures — are people who have moved beyond anger to work against racism in a holistic way. That is MY world. My evolving consciousness and the teachings I receive enable me to live in two worlds.

I once told a non-Native friend who asked me what it was like to go home: It's like taking off one pair of shoes and putting on another pair. Whatever mode of transportation I used to get there, I put behind me what I was involved in — university or a job — to (sometimes involuntarily) remember memories and stories of home.

Because I live away from my family and community, each day is filled with memories and stories. Some days I feel like I'm on a roller coaster. I feel like I'm jumping back and forth between worlds. I find I'm not able to recognize moments of tension,

INTO THE MOON

12

anger, frustration and sorrow as moments when the teachings and values I believe in are attacked, questioned, sometimes ridiculed by Native and non-Native people.

My poetry is my off-spring, symbolically. The words are nurtured by my spirit and then the labour begins. I write about my upbringing and, for the last year, about some of the women in my family. In my culture, the women are the primary teachers. We are matrilineal. Part of my journey and seeking right now is to look at what I've been taught about my history, what I was taught about being a woman and my role in life. My father is a traditional historian and one of my primary teachers. I have begun to write to him, to ask him about our present-day gender roles. How can we say our women have a distinct, important role if we have adopted the western behaviour towards women?

I've written about my grandmother and honoured her teachings about our family, community and responsibilities.

I have a relationship with a non-Native man and I realize, once again, the importance of identity, history, culture and values. For me, it's like I'm blindfolded or we're both blindfolded, having to find a way to walk together.

Gwe Whi

Dawn Ireland-Noganosh

MY NAME IS *GWE WHI* WHICH MEANS *ONE-WHO-GIVES*. THIS NAME was handed down to me. It was my grandmother's name on my father's side. I have just recently learned what this name means. When it was explained to me, it seemed such an appropriate name. It describes my personality to a T, to the point where I have started to resent it.

It seems as though all of my life I have been the one who gives — constantly giving and never getting anything in return. When I feel it's finally my turn, I am afraid to ask for it, or I feel undeserving.

Within the last few years I have been struggling to find my place, my niche, so to speak. I have been struggling with relationships, and have always felt unworthy of anyone's love or kindness. When I am confronted with it, my immediate thoughts are, "You don't REALLY love me — how could you possibly love ME?" or "You only THINK you love me because you don't really know me!" But I also feel, somewhere deep down inside, that I am deserving of a lot better than what I have received in my past relationships. At the same time, I have struggled with letting go and moving on to accepting myself and loving myself.

I feel that I have accomplished some growth. I have been able to look back and see where I have been, and what brought me to that point. I now have the ability to look back and feel good about how far I have come and what I have learned along this trail.

As a certain child once said, "All of the pain and troubles which we go through in life are for a reason, and that reason is to help make us stronger, to prepare us for the role which the Great Spirit has in mind for us."

I Am Seneca

Barbara LaValley

I AM SENECA, IROQUOIS, NEXT TO THE LAST IN A LINE OF WOMEN...

I'm a family member without a nuclear birth family. I know I belong somehow to that group of five girls, one boy, mother and father, but it's such a distant link now that it's little more than a politeness.

My realization that I was a separate being from this family forced its way in when my parents' violence and infidelity precipitated their divorce. I was eight.

I grew up in the care of institutions: in halfway houses and with families of friends. For the next eight or nine years, I existed only in my mind. In my mind I was loved, cared for, beautiful and full of grace. My books were my closest friends.

At eighteen, I married an Ojibwa man. He was twenty at the time and fresh out of Kingston Penitentiary. Those of you who know what it takes to live your life as a "con" will understand some of what drove this man to his eventual death at age twenty-five.

I have one child, a daughter, from my marriage. And she is all that I wish I had been: loved and full of grace. I could not be those things, but I could give birth to them. Success!

Living in the Native community, both urban and rural, has been an addendum to my late adolescence and adulthood. I chose to immerse myself in it rather than leave it behind me. It has been both my pain and my sanity. I have endured the misinformation and negativity allotted to Native peoples by non-Native societies with first confusion, then anger, then fatalism and now hope.

I find I need to change people's perceptions as I define my own. I want to be the end result of my own choosing, not anyone else's.

I am not finished being me, not yet.

A Native Woman

Jane Peloquin

A SINGER, SONGWRITER AND POET, I WAS BORN IN NEW BRUNSWICK. I am a Native woman of the Micmac Nation; I grew up in New Brunswick and different parts of Quebec including Montreal. I later travelled through Canada, living in Calgary and Edmonton for a short time, then in Winnipeg and Toronto. I currently live in Thunder Bay.

I began singing publicly in early 1984 at a coffee house called *Native Expression*. Since then, I have performed at benefits, concerts, coffee houses, cultural festivals, educational institutions, jails, etc.

In 1985, I recorded a cassette tape titled "Believe In Your Dreams." In 1988, I released my second tape, "Don't Forget The Sun." Both tapes contain all original material with 10 songs on each. Both recordings are completely self-financed, self-advertised and self-promoted.

I am currently exploring different forms of writing, such as short stories. In the works for the future, hopefully the near future, are two songbooks to go with my cassette tapes.

I Am

Cat Cayuga

I STAND STILL, TAKE A BREATH AND GIVE THANKS FOR THE LIFE I HAVE been given. I give thanks for the mountains, forests, deserts and jungle I have experienced. I have felt their breath. I give thanks for the waters that have stirred and cooled my soul, the oceans, lakes, and rivers I have swum in. I give thanks for the sunset, sunrises, moonrises and moonsets I have watched from the places I have called home.

When I heard the term "walkabout," which means to walk about the earth to see what there is to see, I felt for this idea. I have done this for a large part of my life. Learning, travelling, connecting with other people of different races and nations on the level of shared humanity, respect and consideration: greater lessons than any institution ever taught me, I have taught myself.

No institution has lifted my curiosity about life to the heights I have achieved on my own. Travelling has taught me to see through eyes of many different colours.

I have also experienced pain, have been abused by the dark side of humanity, but I have always tried to keep my face to the light. It has been a deep understanding of mine since I was young that the Creator has a purpose, a road, a path, a direction for me to walk, which will fulfil my roles, responsibilities and duties — which will allow me to give back all that I have been given.

I am reminded that life is to be lived. This is what I have done — lived with love, pain, fear. All emotions, but I have kept my face toward the light.

WHAT WE DO

An Average Day

Banakonda K. K. Bell

I WOKE WEARY YET GRATEFUL FOR THE NEW DAY — NOT ENOUGH SLEEP, not enough time. Children to wake, dress and feed, to hold and encourage.

Dinner to arrange for the evening, in case of my late return.

Oh dear, I need to do the laundry and I must remember to buy some milk. Oh yes, and tomorrow's Parent's Day. Out to the car, kisses goodbye, have a good day.

On goes the radio: CBC, my companion en route to Toronto to meet my client. God, I need to make my invoice out or I won't get paid!

She's seventeen years old, violent, dangerous, and very hungry for love, love she is afraid to have and afraid to do without. Hungry to learn, but afraid to know — hungry and outright raw with her need.

We meet at the bus station. She's like a little girl smiling shy, "You're on time! Is the moon blue?"

Into my car she climbs with her Walkman and her ghetto-blaster. She's seven now. A moment later as we move into traffic she's in tears.

Long silence — and then out of it a loud angry voice, rolling eyes, twitching cheeks. "You're a slut, a slut just like your no-good mother who couldn't be bothered to bring you up, you're all alike, it's in your blood!" A tiny voice responds out of the same throat, "I'm sorry Mommy."

She turns to me and laughs loud, bouncing undirected, tears fall large, rolling down large cheekbones.

We travel in silence through the country, stopping at a lake. She screams out against her aloneness, begs me to take her home. We stop at a playground and slide, swing and climb. Her laughter is more relaxed. "I feel better now. I need new shoes. Could you get me some batteries for my Walkman?"

It's 5 o'clock, I've got to be home. "Let's go."

We hug and I watch her leave. Turn on my radio. CBC, my companion. Home to my children, my girls. Breathing heavy, focusing on letting go, as tears fall for the lonely girl.

I do "treatment" with her twice a week, two full days.

I say a prayer, and then feel blessed. I turn the corner home. Weary, yet grateful.

Program Assistant

Monica McKay

I WORK FOR A CHURCH ORGANIZATION. PRIMARILY, I PROVIDE ADMIN-
istrative support for the person I work with, who is a Native
man.

The organization where I work is very hierarchical. Titles
mean everything. This same organization, right now, is trying to
work at Pay Equity. The organization tried to make a statement
about working relationships between executives and support staff
by changing the title from secretary to Program Assistant. This
occurred before I took the job, but I try to push it to its fullest
potential.

I work at the Native Ministries office. I answer questions,
telephone calls, and correspondence. I direct people to where
they can get information on social services, on communities, and
on issues such as land claims, education and what involvement
the church has with communities.

I gather information into Resource Kits, and read through
material directed to our desk.

I work creatively on the development and planning of
Gatherings for Natives and non-Natives.

I think that my gifts are acknowledged, but I'm aware that
I make some of the people in the structure uncomfortable when
I talk about equality and the disparity in salaries, and about
power.

Average Workday

Dawn Ireland-Noganosh

*I*HAVE YET TO LEARN WHAT AN AVERAGE WORKDAY IS, BECAUSE I ONLY just started my job three weeks ago and every day has been different so far.

Take last Thursday, for instance. There was an informal meeting with all of the Human Service Providers in our community. We had planned to meet and discuss the upcoming Health Fair. I had invited my friend Bambi, so I could introduce her as a Service Provider with skills that I felt our community could use. The meeting was to commence at 9:00 a.m. in the Resource Centre, but at the last minute it was moved to the boardroom of the Band Administration Office, and, as usual, it didn't actually start until 9:45 a.m. Everyone introduced themselves and explained a little about what their roles were. It was a good opportunity for me to learn about my co-workers' roles and responsibilities, as well as to inform them of my projected activities. Naturally, Bambi couldn't leave without having her say and leaving an impression upon the people there. Would you believe we never got around to talking about the Health Fair?

Afterwards, we enjoyed a nice lunch with a couple of co-workers, one of whom Bambi had worked with previously at Pedahbun Lodge. What a small world!

If this is an example of the average workday, I like it!

Cashier

June Cayuga

MY JOB AS A CASHIER IS NOT CREATIVE, BUT IT'S INTERESTING. IF I had to work without human contact, I think I would quit. Customers become like old friends, telling me about births, marriages, deaths in their families. Great recipes and remedies have been given to me, even a recipe for home-made beer, and I hate beer (even the smell)!

I don't feel that I am undervalued by management or staff. My hours and wages are good. I have heard the odd negative remark about Natives, but it doesn't bother me, because I know who and what I am.

No flowers, please

Barbara LaValley

Money money, no money, owed money...
Are we going to fold or go under?

Budget cuts looming on the horizon for
Native projects, women's programs, social endeavours,
They've become "oh-so-passé" amongst the upper classes,
The voting populace, Strategic Command.

Calls coming in every five minutes...
"Line one, line two!"
"I got it!"
"Can you help me out?"
"I need a job"
"I want to express myself"
"Can anybody answer me, find me work, make me whole?"

Fundraise, strategize, beg, plead, demand...
Politicize, emotionalize, empathize, humanize...
Till you drop dead.

No flowers please.

I Write

Cat Cayuga

I WRITE ANYWHERE, ANYTIME, ANY PLACE, WITH OLD PENS, NEW PENS, broken old pencils that are sharpened with my teeth. I write on any surface material that is available. Napkins, match packets, calendars. I write by firelight, moonlight, daylight, flashlight, houselight. I write by spontaneous combustion.

I write on my civilized kitchen table now and I like it. I write where I am. I write in the wilderness. A computer and an environmentally-safe power supply are on my mind, as an ideal I would like to strive for. I write.

WHAT WE SEE

The following writings were developed by our participants within structured workshop exercises, such as Theme Writing, Beginnings and Endings, Line by Line and Visual Imagery. They are meant to be experimental as well as cooperative, and therefore unique.

I

Joy/JANE/barbara/Joy

Employment Equity — there isn't any

EMPTY CHAIRS FILLED WITH CHEAPER BODIES

a cheaper me, at $4.25 an hour...goddamn!

I have no choice but to live a discounted life.

II

Jane/BARBARA/joy/Jane

The day started with the harshness of rushing, snappy orders,
clipped, unfinished sentences...

TO TOP IT ALL OFF... MY CAT'S HARNESS BROKE IN THE
MIDDLE OF BREAKFAST!

what can one do in a stressed-out, hived-up, harnessless cat
situation

But run in a lumpy, flapping, all-direction state with no exit.

III

Barbara/joy/JANE/Barbara

Pardon me, I'm not quite what you expected,

i may look this way but the real me is undetected

RADAR SCANS THE SURFACE OF MY LEAD ENSHROUDED SELF

I am a part of my continuance of worth.

IV

Jane/BARBARA/joy/Jane

Juices flowing, dripping on messy, cluttered floors
Bits of words bouncing up, the letters are broken, like a jigsaw
puzzle
Three sets of eyes gather to re-assemble the world-altering statement...

"ALPHABETICALLY, THE TERM NATIVE FOLLOWS "INDIAN"
...ANY FURTHER DEFINITION MUST LAG AGAIN"
LETTERS SHAPE WORDS, WORDS SHAPE LANGUAGE,
LANGUAGE SHAPES ME, I SHAPE THE WORLD
THRUSTING, FORCING A NEW ACCEPTANCE OF SELF IN *THIS*
WORLD, I AM A SUM OF LETTERS

sometimes i feel like alphabet soup in a red & white can labelled
"campbells"
i must open that can, remove the label & begin to work with the
cluttered letters inside
occasionally, they form themselves into words in the spoon,
words i can put on and wear like regalia, words like:

Animal
Barbarian
Cree
Death
Equality
Feather
Grandfather
Honour
Indian
Justice
Kettle
Love
"Me"
Nishnawbe
Old One
"Pride"

Say no more.

V

Barbara/JOY/jane/Barbara

I was taught, and taught myself to believe, that the colour of my face was more beautiful in darkness. That I would find acceptance lying down.

FOR SOME REASON, IN THIS WORLD THAT TALKS OF EQUALITY, I HAD BEEN FACED WITH MANY SITUATIONS THAT HAD LEFT ME WANTING TO RIP OFF MY SKIN AND THROW IT AWAY. AN INCREDIBLE CONTRADICTION — THIS SKIN THAT PROVIDED FOR ME MY "CULTURAL COMFORT ZONE" AT TIMES SEEMED MY ENEMY. AND MEN LOOKED AT THIS SKIN, FOUND IT EXOTIC AND TANTALIZING — BUT NEVER COULD MAKE THE CONNECTION THAT UNDER IT LIVED A THINKING, SENSITIVE AND KIND HUMAN BEING...

human! please define
"human"...being...living...breathing...crying...laughing...holding...loving...hating...how i hated my pale skin and craved the ivory tones — but realized that the change from without would never reflect the rich, bright and beautiful colours of my inner rainbow. should i show it? and to whom?

I think I will remain "red"...and rose and peach tones, and let the ivory dreams remain with the elephants. You know, they get slaughtered too.

Mother Earth

Carol Loft

It's funny how I never thought much about her.
How I took her for granted
Until I started searching, understanding.

Now I see the destruction
the pollution, the killing of Mother Earth
Drastic, insidious,
Happening before our eyes, but we don't see
Until we can't escape it.

Mother Earth gives us so much
And we take and take and take
But what have we given in return?
It's time for the people to come
Together in unity
Come together to help save
Mother Earth

Before it really is too late!

Earth Day

Monica McKay

I labour to find the
path to my sacred space
where I am with K'am ligi ahl ahl
I walk daily
to find patches of earth
to walk gently on

There was a time not long ago
I adopted the thinking of
creation being "out there"
that I'd have to wait until my
holidays to go into the "country"

It was at that time that I felt like
I was invisible and imagined myself to
be a balloon, hovering, at the
mercy of the wind

It was at that time that I could not
walk with the elements
I could not give thanks for the rain
because it made my clothes damp
and me uncomfortable

I did not feel rooted, so I allowed
the laws of the concrete jungle to
consume and drive me
I could not journey to my
sacred space, all I found was darkness

I've laboured to find my path
to this place within
In my struggle, my teacher
brought me to her place of peace
and renewal
and I rediscovered water

I felt the wind cleanse me
and the sun warmly caress me
I could feel my spirit being nourished
and I could give thanks

I shed this adopted attitude
and saw creation amidst concrete,
trees reaching upward and outward
fulfilling their responsibility
I could hear the chatter of the bird
and now I walk more slowly
allowing my senses to dance and
honour creation.

Of Earth and Sky

Barbara LaValley

I step out into the dance arena, coming in from the east,
as the sun does...I am in my regalia.
Beads twinkling in the sunlight, tin cones on my dance cape
meshing together in sound as they sway.

My hair is braided tightly, too tightly,
though I know it will loosen with the day
as will my moccasins and my beaded belt...

The wind stirs up a fine dust that settles on my face and hands,
mingling with the sweat to form a film of crusty salt.
It protects me from the burning of the sun,
but will sting when I wash it away, later.

My feet feel every clump of grass not stamped down by others,
every stone and twig left unswept.
I pass over them in my atonement,
a small price to pay for being able to dance...
as is the weariness that will come.

Other dancers glide by me, some fast, some slow.
Some laughing, talking to friends, while others
like me, are silent and intent
I watch with hopeful eyes, questioning eyes,
the traditional women dancers. They are substance.
Smooth and wrinkled faces emanating some fuller knowledge
than I.
One approaches...

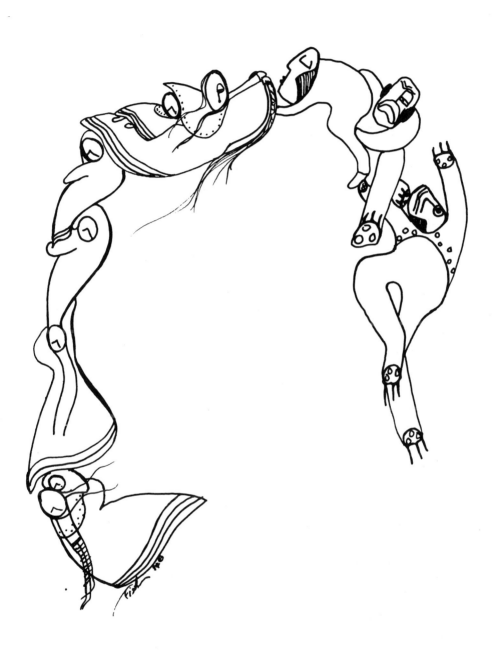

INTO THE MOON

One approaches...

"I like the way you dance," she says, "are you from around here?"

"No," I say, and hang my head. "I am not from this place,
but another, far away and distant to me now."

"It is the same with me," she says, smiling.

"How do you seem so at ease then, so content?" I wonder aloud,
"I can't."
"Put your eyes in the very tops of the trees...just over there,
ahead of you... and let your feet enter the ground, just below the
surface, not more than an inch or two, lest you root yourself and
fall," she said with a smile, "feel the earth between your toes,
let yourself become one with the soil and wind. Then, you will
feel at home."

I am grateful, for her time,
and for her words,
for her being there with me.
I am of earth, and sky too...I belong here.

Poem

Cat Cayuga

Fire, warmth, rhythmic tones
I sense you

Hand thrust deep into heart
I feel you

Blood, drinking, your blood
I live you

Closed, eyes, pain, hurt, wounds
I scream with you

Sleep, safety, dreaming
I love you and give thanks
(I give thanks and love you)

Poem

June Cayuga

Trees bent and broken

Struggling for survival

Lakes and rivers

Brown sludge

Earth Day

Are we too late?

Never

What has been

Can be again

Without Beauty

Monica McKay

I wish for you
a life without beauty.

I could laugh and love freely.

You have stolen that from me,
just as you silently assaulted
my spirit.

You coward! Your spirit must
torment you, for spirit is
pure and feeling.

In silence you attacked my spirit.
You have wrestled and broken
my respect and worth.

My soul quietly sings a death chant,
in the midst of that
is a song of war.

My spirit is wounded.

I am broken...
but I will live.

The Calling

Lee Johns

The time is upon us
Did they not let you know?
Or were you not listening,
And thought the stories too old?

The true ways of our people
Have been humble and meek,
Mistaken by others as lazy and weak.
Get ready, people, our time is at hand
The Peace our Grandfather envisioned
Is unfolding as planned.

Our Mother is sick, in pain and despair,
She calls to her children who don't seem to care
Her body is poisoned, tired and weak
She's afraid for the life she can no longer keep

As the night falls upon us
And there's darkness all 'round
Remember your Mother, from whom you will run
Grandfather will help in Her new coming birth
And the world will no longer see Her as just dirt.

Come gather your bundles of Medicines and Sage
And walk into the dawning of this new age
Come, heal your hearts and dry your eyes
A time once spoken of has now arrived.

INTO THE MOON
47

Clear the Way for Technology

Lee Johns

I see
natural beauty
cut up and left to rot.

I take a deep breath.

It reminds me of women
treated with the same disrespect
as Earth Mother is.

In the distance, I see a stand
of Grandfather trees, old trees,
old forest. Peace was
there before man began
cutting away to clear
the way for technology.

In the distance, the formation
partially hidden by the mist
outlines the form of truth,
that it is Woman.

I see my mother
lying there raped.

Variation I

Lee Johns

I see
devastation of
natural beauty,
cut down like the
rainforest,
the very life struggles to live.
A deep breath,
in the distance, a formation
partially formed yet hidden by mist,
a maiden earth lies stretched, grieving
and motionless of all life, death of
grandfather trees cut and lying
on the breast that nourished
and no further thought of
the beautiful life that
technology devastates
takes what was
so that it
will never
ever be
again.

This Picture of Trees

Banakonda K. K. Bell

I LOOK AT THE PICTURE: STUMPS AND UNVALUED BRANCHES LYING LIKE debris. Beyond, the trees are barren, grow barely, look feeble, though they are young. A hydro line strings down from the barren pole. No need for hydro any longer; the chainsaw's work is done.

The forest is scarred and bruised. The evergreens in the distance trembled with the aching earth, witnessing the ravage, and now are waiting.

One tree — tall, thin — is left standing alone. Who knows why? It sways in the breeze as it mourns the disturbed ecology which floods its roots with toxins.

It makes me think of when I had my pubic hair shaved off, when I birthed my firstborn. I had been bullied by procedure and I cried out against the indignity and pain. In the following weeks, it went from stubble back to its familiar growth. Sterility its purpose, yet denied its results. Like the denial of the forest, our relative, and of our need for its survival.

I always hear talk of humans and nature as if we are separate. When will it be spoken — the truth of our existence? We are NOT separate. Our umbilical cord is still attached to this Mother Earth. Our future does not exist without it.

I feel tears. I feel anger. A voice from deep inside calls, "Stop, stop! My Grandmother's Grandmother left this for us. We must leave it for our children's children."

Clearcut

Monica McKay

It is difficult to look at an open wound
especially if it is infected
I wonder how it came to be?
an act of violence? an accident?
was it meant to be?

In the silence these questions hang.

Will it leave a scar?
How deep is it?
I see no way
to help the healing.

Yet I cannot look at pain and not
be moved to feel.

I will wait and allow you all the time you need
to tell your story
I will follow your lead
and together we will learn the importance
of our relationship.

"If a tree falls in the forest, does anybody care?"
a line by a songwriter...

I cannot hear the forest's story, just yet.
But we're interfering with its responsibility
taking its life in disrespect
An act of violence.
And we are blind and mute to its pain.

INTO THE MOON
53

Trees

Barbara LaValley

"Can't see the forest for the trees..." Well, not anymore

Like deadwood, fallen branches, we who remain
hover in the background, clinging to the mountains

Ah, the cedars, those medicine trees,
healthy only at the tops now...like we.
They wither, and cannot grow upward.

"Clear out the underbrush... get rid of the excess!" So you say.

"Take what you need and leave the rest," I say.

What grows has life, purpose —
Not to fulfil our wrapping, packaging, toiletry needs,
but to cleanse the air, provide shelter and give warmth.

Talk to them of your relationship to the earth.
Mould to the rough bark, let trees comfort you.
Do not kill or maim your life's breath
for trees sustain the movable.

Man-made Disease

Dawn Ireland-Noganosh

What drives you to do this to my body?
Once, you thought I was beautiful
Now you take the very strength that you admired
when you first came.

I gave of myself to you, freely, trusting you.
You told me that I could trust you,
that you would never
do anything to hurt me.

Look at me
look at what you've done to me.
Where there was once only beauty
now scars remain for your possession.

Standing

Cat Cayuga

Stick-standing people —

I see you in fields of slaughter,

Corporate interests, and the ignorant,

Imagine your lives

to be nothing more than paper.

Can I turn your pain

To beauty, give life, return respect

to your spirits

By giving my spirit to this pen

So others can share your sacrifice?

The balance is to be experienced

between paper and pen.

There Has to be Balance

June Cayuga

What the future holds:

Humans have ravaged the forests

As humans have ravaged humans.

Thoughtlessness towards humans and nature

Begins to show on our planet.

Industrial growth, jobs

Seem to be more important

Than the natural habitat or

the living creatures of the forest.

We know there has to be a balance

Between humans and nature.

Forests, refuges of quiet serenity

Personal growths, are lost

Memories to reclaim.

Mother's Pride

Dawn Ireland-Noganosh

She watches the hawk gliding briefly overhead
       and thinks of her son
Pride fills her heart.
She thought of him
       when he was yet unborn
She remembers how she would lie awake at night
       staring at the empty crib
waiting...

for the boy
she knew
she was carrying inside her
Born
Finally
Her son.

Watching him grow,
to become a traditional dancer
Honoured with an eagle feather
       by the Elder,
for his hunger to learn the old ways.
They danced for him
       an honour song,
a symbol of their pride
       and joy in him,
she was filled with this emotion.

A singer now
        with the drum
he learns the old songs.
She listens intently
as they sing
        their honour song
for her.

It's time now
        for the women's circle
and with her head held high
        so full of pride,
she walks up the road.

Survivor

Carol Loft

She watched the hawk gliding overhead
This brought back many memories.
Memories of the time when she was young,
still on the reserve.

What she remembered most
was being shunned by the kids at school.
Why did they treat her so cruelly?
Was it because she dressed differently?
Because she spoke with an accent?
Because her skin was dark?
She was never sure why.

Her parents told her she had to go to the whiteman's school
There was nothing for her on the reserve
They wanted better for her,
that she would fly like the hawk, that she would be strong,
That she would survive.

Well, she got through the school,
but not without bitterness,
She worked in the whiteman's world,
but not without being used, betrayed and hurt,
over and over.

She was back home now and broken...

her spirit subdued.
She wondered what her parents would think
if they could see her now.

She took one last glance at the hawk,
shrugged her shoulders,
drank the last dregs of her wine,
threw the bottle into the ditch and walked up the road.

The Walk

Monica McKay

S HE WATCHED THE HAWK GLIDING OVERHEAD. SHE NOTICED THAT THE sun was beginning to set and the purple-red fingers were gently caressing the tops of the hills and trees. She wondered how long she'd walked. She felt relaxed and warm after walking so quickly, not caring what lay in her path.

When she first started to walk, it was as if she was late for an appointment. Nothing mattered, but the walking. Her body jolted as she tripped; her feet tangled in fallen branches. Untangling herself, she stood and could smell the packed dirt and plant life, kind of musky. Her feet felt the earth moving to accommodate her steps. Her foot was pulled gently towards the ground, then released. She had a sudden urge to take her shoes off, but she wanted to get to the lake before dark.

She felt anticipation, and walked quickly. She came into the clearing and looked at the flatness of the surface of the water. The pebbles and rocks beneath her feet reverberated in a rhythmic, crunching noise.

She bent down and looked slowly around, not knowing what it was she was searching for. She picked up a bright rust-red stone. Looking at it closely, she wondered what colour it would be when it dried. It felt good. It filled up the spaces when she closed her hand.

Then her feet began to take her in the direction of the road. Reluctantly, she walked up the road.

Winged Shadows

Barbara LaValley

She watched the hawk gliding overhead
Its wings casting shadows upon her face
Spiralling upward, it banked.
Though far away, she swore she saw its eye gleaming
at her.

It seemed to know her thoughts
and was not afraid
that the woman wanted it, had sought it
for its power and its blessing.

Bands in its tail-feathers flashing red
brought kinship of her Grandfather's clan
and like William of before
acknowledged her right to know of him...

Circling the rock-face studded with black spruce,
cedar, lichen and scrub-pine,
it cried out a warning of things to come...
It/he would not "change shape"
or bare its eye in recognition again
instead, it left a feather to remind her.

Gathering her things, she shouldered her bag
of rocks and the feather
and clambering back down the bluff,
set her wings beneath her clothing and walked up the road.

Where You Fly I Fly

Cat Cayuga

SHE WATCHED THE HAWK GLIDING OVERHEAD. LOWERING HER GAZE, she stood still — planted, like the trees that surrounded her. Closing her eyes, remembering her sister, she imagined herself as part, as one with her. Breathing deeply. Concentrating. Down. One, zero, alpha, nothing.

Fluttering. She lifted her eyes and wings to the sky, trying to follow, catch up to her sister. "Wait!" she yelled (or so she thought). Sound echoing over the hills, vibrating off the trees and streams, back to her. Panic. She thought herself to be alone. Sister flew the circle, returned to her side. Together they flew, spiralling, feeling the wind like it had never felt. Soon, she took chances, tempting fate, playing with destiny. She'd never felt so alive.

Then where was her sister? She began to falter, wings no longer strong (or so she thought). Her voice was a moan to her heart, falling like a stone; she had forgotten how to fly alone.

Blackness. It was as if she had been hit by something larger than herself. Her mind and body hurt, eyes burned from the brightness of the sun. Focus. Soon everything was as it should be. She watched the hawk gliding overhead. Smiling, turning, she walked up the road.

A Lesson from Nature

June Cayuga

She watched the hawk gliding overhead.

Free to explore, free to look down on earth's splendour

Free to see a worldly view of life's busy and quiet times.

She stopped, for a moment, and realized that down here

she could have this freedom by becoming in tune

with her mother, the Earth.

Tucked in its beak the hawk had its meal for the day —

no more than it needed, no less.

She wondered: why can't humankind take this lesson?

She walked quietly, freely, down the road.

WRITE SPACES

The Place I Write

Dawn Ireland-Noganosh

Late at night when everyone has gone to sleep
and I, wishing I could do the same,
am lying awake, tossing and turning
with thoughts flooding my brain

He is crying out to me, "Talk to me!"
and as much as I try to ignore him
He won't be silent

I sit up in my antique bed,
discovered at a local flea market,
and switch on the soft light.
The stained-glass lamp
uncovered from someone else's junk-pile
sits on my treasured pedestal.
I entertain the idea

In the sanctuary of my bedroom, I retreat
amongst my treasures
when I find the need to escape and find refuge
from the chaos of those outside forces
which impose themselves upon my existence

When I close the door it's just me

Alone with him and he keeps insisting
"Talk to me and together we'll walk through it,
and come to an understanding of something we can live with."

That wretched journal has found his way into my heart again
It's rare that he hears from me of late
I take that as a good sign
for I rest more peacefully these days

Out of Chaos

Carol Loft

The times that I write are few and far between
  When I do put something on paper
    It's to get rid of frustrating,
      confusing,
        angry or
          hopeless,
            hopeless,
              hopeless feelings

Usually after I have felt much anger at my family,
    or worse yet, have yelled at my kids or husband

I go into my bedroom, sit on the floor
    and write, Write, WRITE
Until I'm empty, exhausted and placated for
    the time being
At these times, pen and paper save me
    Until the next time

My Workspace

Monica McKay

MY WORKSPACE IS LARGE. MY DESK IS LARGE AND THE WALLS surrounding my desk are filled with Native art and posters with inspiring words from Native people.

On a shelf above my desk I have some rocks, and some small boxes from Central America. It's wonderful to have the rocks, because I need to hold, caress and squeeze and stare at them as I move the words to new places on the monitor.

I would like to re-create this space at home. A sacred space. A place to be alone and safe in.

My Workspace / Where I Write

Barbara LaValley

MY WORKSPACE IS EITHER ON MY KITCHEN TABLE WITH AN OLD office typewriter that doesn't correct itself, or in the office on the IBM compatible during lunch hour... or during stolen time on a quiet day.

I got in trouble at my last job for writing during work-time. I WAS on a break, but my boss said, as she snuck up on me and leaned over my shoulder, that what I was doing wasn't work-related. She chewed me out, embarrassed me in front of my co-workers. So I quit moonlighting at my writing, though it IS more exciting when it's "stolen time."

Every once in a while I'll go through an extreme period of writing — I'll stay up all night to get a story down on paper... not as often as I should though.

I would like to have a quiet room all set up with a picture window, desk, computer terminal and supplies. Somewhere that is entirely mine. Maybe when I move into a larger space this summer... as a matter of fact, I'm going to make it a priority.

STRENGTH

Into the Moon

Barbara LaValley

I see a face in the sky and I imagine it to be mine
reflecting sorrow or happiness as I choose.

My body is swollen and tender to the touch
It is your Moon, my mother tells me.

Mine? Yes, truly mine, for years I have thought so...
this "sister" who helps me to feel, belongs to me

Come, gather your things. We will build you shelter.
Aunties gather around me and whisper secrets...

Remembering their own times, they direct me
as I sweat, as I bathe, prepare food and clothing.

No man may touch you now, not even a fingertip,
You are too powerful, you must be careful.

No father's embrace? No brother's playfulness?
No. They are incomplete. Unfinished. Vulnerable.

Who will I have when you leave me here? I am afraid.
You have your Moon to keep you company, inside and above you.

She is the first of us, female and strong...
she pulls water from the earth and blood from our bodies.

She tells us when to plant a seed, when to give birth, when to die.

She will help you to be her counterpart here, amongst men.

She will never leave you.

I am shy to be left with her, my friend, though I believe.
I will sleep and walk this night into the moon.

Giigs

Monica McKay

Giigs, my heart misses you.
My body and soul
ache to hold you close.

Across all the miles, it is not hard
to join with you, in my mind.

From our beginning we knew the power that was
given to the women of the Nisga's Nation. We are
Life-givers, life-sustainers, providers, teachers.
Within us is the power to re-create life.

I have heard the wisdom that you possess and
that your wisdom is recognized and respected.
You stand as matriarch in the house of Bil'.

You know the property rights our house has
and is blessed with.
You know the names that belong to our house,
and as caretaker, have never considered this your right.

You are strong like the river, who provides for us.
Like her, your strength is demonstrated
in the gentleness that comes from your very soul.
The currents beneath the surface
are like the ideals by which you live life.

When she is turbulent, you are angry

Has someone tried to hurt
one of your family?
But your family is not just you, it is all of us.
It is the way of life you have instilled in us.

If I look into the mirror I do not see
my reflection alone,
I see my family, my tribe, my people,
I am not alone...

Look at me.

Of Be(long)ing

Barbara LaValley

The woman shivers, stepping into the cold.
Flesh tingling, unsure in her perceptions,
She waits for an opportune moment to speak
to the one who has led her there.

The maw extends to caress, to assist her
as she lowers herself onto its curling hide
complete, with long fibres of emotional depth
contented with its rhythmic warmth.

Stifling heat, sticky wetness, salty film on tongue and eye.
No one had told her it would be so all-encompassing,
this foray into "belonging to," "spousal accord."
She is unable to shift or alter outcome.

To change the patterns set by others, the woman talks,
of lives and loves, fidelity and trust — endemic values.
Sensing in the midst of this, her time nearly over
"Well then," she says, and slays the beast.

From Loneliness

Cat Cayuga

I don't want to write you, the poem that will separate
my heart, with my own pain.

I want to be safe inside an abstract pen, disguising the ache

I am afraid of the sensation of being touched, of opening coffins
long sealed and shut.

When I was a child and wind blew from my mouth, I imagined
myself immortal and untouchable.

In my youth on cool summer nights, I would wrap myself
with the stars and ride on my horse...

I never thought that I would bleed from loneliness,
that time would become a razor.

Wounded, I circle my lodge of objects that measure my life,
objects.

Wounded, bleeding, lying on my side, painting old dreams,
I never thought that I would bleed from loneliness.

My time, now, is a river, with old photographs floating.
I reach for them with limp hands, remembering.

STORIES TO TELL

Dance Til You Wake

Jane Peloquin

AWAKENING HAPPENS ANY TIME, ANY PLACE, WHEN YOU LEAST EXPECT it. It comes to you through people previously unknown. Minds and hearts seek commonalities; smiles crease faces — replacing frowns caused by feelings of isolation. Why is it? they ask each other, as they strive to reach into the centre of the other, probing for that seed of knowing knowledge. How do I find it? Where does it end? Is it really as bad as I feel?

Walking alone among the arrogant and irreverent, I am small and lost, falling prey to those who claim superiority and wisdom in their values, looking up into a face filled with venom. Striving for such complete control must be exhausting!

Can I see inside those angry eyes once my ears are filled with sage, smouldering, smudging my brain? Spirit helpers creep into my peripheral vision, shadowy visions dancing with joy and celebration on the edge of my spirit self. Their childlike prancing brings a cautious smile to my lips as the tumbling words from thin, dry lips fall helter-skelter on the air. The song they are singing is filled with words I cannot understand but feel as a tug in my chest, a swelling surrounding my heart, protective wrapping. The crescendo builds until the angry sounds are muffled, buried in the ball of mist coming from the dancers, encircling the will and effort of the desperately desperate trying to wash my mind of all that is my truth.

Anger becomes heavier and heavier — no recipient to carry it away. Without relief it turns in upon itself and feeds the maelstrom inside. I almost feel sad — almost feel guilty — almost waver and give myself over to the temptation to rescue. I tried to listen to the words again, tried to nod understanding, tried to find compassion, tried to offer comfort to the coldness radiating from the body where I stood before. But the cold Arctic wind offers no opportunity for the compassionate to warm its icy core. The self-proclaimed will claim the prize of accomplishment. The air quivers with the breath of the bag of bones, eyes growing dull. Finally the lips are still, cracked and hanging limply.

I walked out from under the clouds, blink away the mist and dance.

That Cousin

Cat Cayuga

I WONDER ABOUT LOVE. THE KIND THAT YOU HARBOUR, CREATING AN ideal of that lover, the one who makes your pants moist, but in the dream you never see his face. I think it is best this way. Then any man can be the man in the dream who makes your pants wet. I came from a family that showed no affection or emotion, so I wasn't one of those excessively cute kids. People like those cute kids who give them hugs and make them feel good about themselves at that moment. As if the kid only hugs excessively nice people. I didn't like to be touched, hugged, stroked or kissed, it was strange for me.

Once, a cousin of mine was babysitting, and he was playing hide and seek with me and my brother. He took me to hide on the cellar-landing, while my brother Freeman counted to ten. Cellars remind me of families that don't touch, because they are dark and hold lonely secrets. Anyway, I was lying with this cousin of mine, waiting for Freeman to find us, and he started to touch my body. It was not the kind of touch that feels good. It was the kind of touch that made me feel confused and ashamed. He put his hands in my pants and kept touching. I didn't know what to do. I was only four years old. I didn't want my brother to see. I just jumped up and felt his hand slip out of my pants and along my body; the touch felt like thorns. I avoided that cousin all night, but near bedtime I began to worry. I knew that the cellar-landing was only the beginning.

I kept checking the clock and my heart to see if they were both still working. That cousin didn't try anything, but I wasn't fooled. I could see the thorns on his hands. I knew they needed blood — my blood. I lay in bed terrified. Ghosts and all those childhood fears were not as great as the fear I felt waiting for the thorns to grow.

"Come and play," he told me. I said I was too tired and was going to sleep. "Come and play!" that cousin told me, with the mock authority of an adult. In the light from the living room his face seemed to blend with the darkness of the room, making him dangerous.

I jumped across the bed. "No," I yelled. "No, no, no!" That cousin grabbed my arm and tried to pull me over the bed frame. "I will tell," I screamed. "I am going to tell!" That cousin let go of my arm and told me to shut up and go to sleep. As he walked away he laughed, and told me no one would believe me.

I wondered if my brother was awake in the top bunk and scared like me. I wonder if that cousin touched my brother when he played with him. That cousin baby-sat all my cousins. Everyone liked him and thought he was great with kids.

I told my mother and she was mad. She wanted to tell everyone what he was like and what he might be doing to their children. My dad told her not to be crazy. That cousin was his sister's son. What did my dad care? He was always drunk, and he beat my mother. My mother phoned that cousin and told him if he ever came around or touched me she would kill him, and if he touched any of my cousins and she heard about it, she would kill him. I don't think she would really kill him. But I will tell you something, I would. I would kill that cousin.

Discovery

Barbara LaValley

*T*HERE WERE A SERIES OF EVENTS THAT LED UP TO THE FIRST, WORST day of my life. I have experienced other days since that rivalled it in intensity, but none contained the first knowledge of that October 15th, 1970.

I had been residing, much against my will, at a state-funded halfway house with the ignominious title of "Discovery House." At the time, it was the only such residence in the New England area aside from Covenant House in New York City, a drug rehabilitation centre for young offenders. Discovery House was a state-funded and licensed "alternative development" that took in people who'd had trouble with the law, rather than send them to the state reformatory.

My arrival in this place had been engineered by my mother, supported by fictitious accounts of my many transgressions. She, at the time of my parents' second divorce, had been granted custody of the three youngest children in our family. I, being second youngest and a girl, was not wanted by my father. My brother was luckier.

There was a shakedown in "house infrastructure" happening that day, and my name and history came up for review.

Being a naive 13-year-old, I was under the long-standing belief that grownups would somehow be there to take care of me...no matter what.

When they told me that I would never live with or see my mother again, I did not want to believe them. When they showed me the letter and the signed custody agreement that they said she had voluntarily provided, I cried.

As they spoke to me of the minimum two-year intern-
ment I would be facing, I looked out of the window.

It had been raining off and on since early morning. As my
tears dried, the rain cried for me.

I knew that what I had long suspected was true: my
mother had never loved me in the way I had tried to believe she
would.

The realization came that I was without parentage.

Turtledream

Cat Cayuga

PINS — FRIGID, SILVER PINS — PROTRUDING FROM MY TONGUE. Wake, wake.

Black robes are descending upon me trying to eat my language, eat my voice, grasp my heart, smother my spirit.
Wake, wake.

I tumble, reeling, searching for a way home, a way out of this dream. In the distance there is luminous green. It is the turtle. I scream, blood runs down my chin. The pins have been placed. I screech with my heart, wait. I cry with my spirit, you know me, I am your daughter.
Wake, wake.

Rough cloth, wool, is touching, scratching my body. I am drowning in darkness.
Wake, wake.

* * *

Time is held within a seed as the turtle turns and acknowledges my presence, as I suffocate in ebony. I meet those eyes that hold creation, those eyes observing my pain, those eyes just watching. I am cloaked in blackness.
Wake, wake, wake up.

I come alive. I am in the world I know. Blankets are twisted around my body like a straitjacket. Quickly, I untangle myself and get out of bed. It is starting to look like an enemy, not the friend I crave. Sleep is death. How many times can my spirit die?

I want to be hugged, reassured that I am not prancing in a Salvador Dali dream, but there is no one. No Mother — she took the aqua azul as a lover, never to walk in air again. No Father — he put on his Indian boots and walked into the west. (I wonder if he loved us or the original Woman who walked into the blood of Mother Earth, who walked into the water because of the pain he gave.)   No brother, no sisters, they were taken to the cave of bureaucracy never to be seen again.

My breath tastes of black bile. The spasm in my chest is thunder. My legs will no longer hold the weight of the pain. The room begins a dance tribute to the cosmos. I don't want to dance. I struggle to keep my delicate grip in this world, but it is too late.

My body is toxic. Remembering is not my real fear. I fear losing my sanity in dream. I begin to fall.

The funeral is small, just Mom's immediate family. The day is clear and blue, like the water she drowned in, clear, blue irony. Maybe Mom would have thought it funny. She had a sense of humour. While other Mothers had their children bring willow branches to snap across behinds, Mom usually found comedy in our antics. This was one of her gifts.

I am wearing the yellow and blue-ribbon dress Mom made for me; it is now my most treasured belonging. Tasson is beside me in his russet three-piece suit. He looks like a three-year-old man. The sun is spiralling off the top of his head, making his hair bluish-black. (I have nondescript brown hair.) He is unsure of what is happening. And no matter how many times I explain the situation, he thinks Mom is coming home. He trusts her.

Beside Tasson is Katsi. She is ten, and comprehends death. She is pretending that she is not affected by this change in our lives, pretending that everything is within her control. I think Katsi may grow up to have a martyr personality. It will give her the attention she desires, and needs. I hope this never comes true. Martyrs need pain for worth. She is beautiful, her dark skin is highlighted by the beads of sweat that this day and its sun bring. (I have nondescript yellow skin.)

Zeeta's hands are fluttering in front of my face, like two small hummingbirds. Zeeta is our special child, she hears the world through her hands. Her dad thought she was more of a curse than special, a black hole in his sainted manhood. How could his sperm have had a hand in creating the hummingbird child? Zeeta has eyes as black as a night when our Grandmother moon does not shine her light. They express her life, voice her feelings. (I have nondescript blue-green-grey eyes.)

Auntie Bea is faking grief, the same way some fake orgasm. Only she is better. She is spouting all those funeral clichés and gives the impression she is a professional mourner. "Oh, so young. Such a poor woman. What will become of the poor children?" She knew what would become of us but did nothing. She performs a true visionary piece of melodramatic acting, her arm hanging pathetically across her face as she manoeuvers her pounds of decaying flesh onto a chair. The chair breaks.

I laugh, I can't stop laughing. People are looking at me as if I should be shamed into the ground. It serves her right, I want to scream, after all the cruelty she has heaped on our family.

I look into the grave hoping that death will control the laughter. It is the first time I experience the slipping, falling, losing-balance feeling. It is the first time I see the turtle. It is in Mom's grave looking up, looking at me. I am drawn into the eyes, tunnels that take me to life, to time. Mom is standing there asking me to promise that I will be the new mother.

"I can't," I whine, "I'm too young."

"Promise me," she says.

"They will never let a sixteen-year-old do it."

"Promise me," she says.

"I'm so small, so helpless."

"Promise me."

I promise her.

★   ★   ★

My face is on cold tile. The floor looks like it could use a good wash. I wake up this way, face on the floor, deciding it needs a good wash, as if by thinking this stupid thing, I will forget. I will forget my promise.

I get up. My arm hurts. The clock on the wall gives me no indication of how long I have been gone. Someday I will try and time myself. I am grateful it rarely happens in public. The pills I get from the doctor are supposed to stop these "Victorian vapours".

When these "episodes", as I call them, first started, I imagined myself to be blessed by the trickster spirit; that I was half-female, half-ghost. I walked in two worlds to sort the confusion, the guilt.

The guilt is the worst. After the funeral I had no speech to tell of our betrayal by Auntie Bea, the broken promises. We were not going to be all together. I could not look at their eyes, with my head turned from them. I could feel their spirits touching mine, seeking answers I didn't have. Did they know about the promise I had made? Is it why they were touching me? It was then that I understood the vision at the grave.

We were fragmented by a destructive child throwing the pieces of the puzzle to the wind, not caring where the pieces landed, not caring that the puzzle could never be put together again.

My contact with the others the first couple of years was as a mother of distance. This is the best I can do until I am older I would tell the walls, chair, anything that would listen. I lost their directions as I began to lose myself. Wandering from place to place, never staying long enough to make connections, friendships, just long enough to confirm my fragile existence.

In the beginning, I would dream that Tasson, Katsi, Zeeta and I replaced the stars, forming a circle. And in the middle would be Mom and, at times, the turtle. It was reassuring, but I fell off the edge of the world, having held on only with my fingernails. The dreams began to remind me of the pain in my heart.

Katsi had been saved. I am the martyr, Saint Someone-or-

Other, a holy Indian following the black robe, abandoning my own people, my family as if they were worth nothing. At night I lie on a blanket of thorns, thrashing, calling all to my pain. My physical self is nothing. I am accumulating savings for my spiritual self to get to "heaven."

I whip myself in the light, my blood a stark contrast to the beauty around me. I no longer see beauty. I see black and pain. I walk with a beauteous smile, telling my story to sympathetic ears that want light, and darkness to those who would gladly carry it. My story is my manipulative tool, embellished to get what I want.

I make myself sick. I am nauseated in the middle of the room I call home, my total worth a pathetic attempt to mask poverty behind a bohemian facade.

I need to get out. I am the snake. The room is the fire burning the African plain, my body slithers from the tongues of yellow, red and gold. The fire burns faster than I can travel. The brush on fire is a mad person dancing, dancing on my body. I open my mouth and only blood flows out. I need to be out of this room.

On the street the sun is in my eyes, making the world bright. I take a pair of interesting, overpowering, and in no way subtle vintage sunglasses out of my pocket. I like these old things. Looking through them, I know no one can see in. I like it this way.

Walking, seeing only the barest traces of life. Never seeing anything in so much detail that I could describe it. The dreams are enough for me. Walking, walking away from the city core, toward the tree.

When I was little, there was a tree I would sit in and read. The branches would cradle my body. One day I came home to find that Hydro had cut the tree, because it was in the way of the wires. Humans were in the way of that tree and it never complained. Look what it got for its silence.

Once again the pain in my chest is thunder. I fumble in

my pockets for my vapour pills. I swallow them without water. They taste like dry bird crap. It's a funny saying people have — who has actually eaten shit and can compare other tastes to it?

I smell and see the trees. It is a beautiful stand, but doomed to someday be a mall or a convenience store. I shake my head. Don't be cynical, I tell myself. It would be a good place to die. I laugh to myself as I spout off the stoic Indian innuendo that forms white people's perception of who we are.

I lie under a tree and look at the canopy of green and blue over my head. The grass is soft and caresses my legs and arms. Wondering where it came from, I feel a tear on my cheek. I rescue it with my tongue.

My Uncle Max once said that we are cousins to the ocean because of the water we carry, that our bones are made of minerals similar to the sea. As infants in the womb, we grow in water which is soon perceived by the baby to be steam, like the steam in the sweat lodge. The tear with its salty taste reminds me of that teaching, long ago. Closing my eyes I imagine myself to be the baby in the steam; the heat of the day helps my imagination.

Pain: frigid silver pins protruding from my tongue. Someone is gently taking them out. I hear them drop onto wool. I see Mom standing in front of me. She has taken all of the pins out. My voice now belongs to me.

I can't look at her — I am so ashamed of what I have become, and of my promises not kept. "I am sorry," I tell her. "All the things you taught me, all the strength you tried to instill in my spirit. I abused it all — I am sorry."

She reaches out and hugs me. Her touch is solid. I am confused. I don't remember dreaming. I panic. Has my sanity become lost in dream?

Mom senses my fear, takes my hand as we walk down the tunnel of the turtle's eyes.

Monologue

Jane Peloquin

SEE MY HAND, HOW IT SHAKES? IT'S NOT NORMAL. IS IT? BEEN LIKE that ever since I got sick. A year now. They did every test in the book. Oh, it's awful. Wouldn't want to go through that again. Even had that CAT scan test? They said it's nerves. Have you ever felt fear? It's the fear that makes me nervous. A year ago I wouldn't stay alone, you know. It started when I got sick.

George drank a 40-ouncer of rye in two days. Wouldn't you say that's a lot? They said he could have two ryes in two days. He's not sticking to his quota. It started when I got sick, a year ago. He gets nasty now when he drinks. You can't say anything to him. He just has another rye. He says things that I can never forgive him for — never. Now's when we should be doing things together.

Well, I won't keep you. I know you're busy. So talented. You did your laundry already? And made muffins? I don't know where you get your energy. Me, I just don't feel myself any more. Even at work, they say I've changed. To tell you the truth, I just don't give a sh— to be honest with you, a shit any more.

I'm not, you know, conscientious like I used to be. You know, you don't even have to look at the clock. Twelve, twelve-thirty he starts. I hear him at the ice cubes, and still drinking at six. One of them bottles of rye cost $27.95. And he's mad because I didn't give him nothing towards his new jeans. Went and bought them himself.

Well I won't keep you. I know you're busy. Will you be home tomorrow night? I'll leave you the key. I'll likely be in bed by the time you get home, if you're going out. To tell you the truth, sometimes I'm in bed by eight-thirty. Anyway, if you can let Murphy in, that would be good. If I let him in now, he'll have me up at five in the morning. He wanted to come in this afternoon but I wouldn't let him. He'd only sleep, then want to stay out late. I'm not going to sit up and wait for him.

George sits there and acts like his doorman. Of course, he sits there and drinks 'til all hours. I know he's drinking right out at camp. Of course they all do. And they go out in the boat, too. Yesterday, he drank half a bottle of rye before supper. Then he had another one after supper and in his cooler I saw five cans of beer. That'll all be gone before he gets up there. Drinks in the car now. They said he could have two ryes a day. He's not sticking to his quota. He drank a 40-ouncer of rye in two days. That's a lot, don't you think? I think so. Not to mention the beers. He was in the hospital and they know he was overdoing it. Said they could tell by his blood. They asked me how much he drank but I didn't want to say anything, you know. They told him he could have two a day and that's all.

I was at the doctor's today. I told him about my fears. I told him I was scared the cancer was back. He said it was nerves. You know, I only weigh a hundred and two now. It's my head I'm worried about. The other night I thought it would burst it hurt so bad. The doctor said I could tell by my, you know, going to the bathroom. To be honest with you, I've always had trouble with being constipated. I took a Feenamint the other day and was running to the bathroom like crazy.

But anyway, the family knows that George and me are ... you know. He's even put them down, and his one and only son. I don't know how he could do that. We're lucky he's still alive after the car accident. He's still not completely back to normal. He doesn't drink anymore, since the accident. All because of a party. They were all friends. His best friend got killed. And George puts him down. Says I'm turning the family against him. He doesn't realize he's doing it himself. When he starts drinking, I just go down in the basement. I stay out of his way. And who would want to go to bed with someone who's three sheets to the wind? You're supposed to make love with someone in that condition?

Not me! No way.

I think he knows I've lost certain feelings for him. This is between you and me. If George found out, he'd kill me. He's getting more nasty all the time when he's drinking. He's never hit me or anything like that — not yet anyway. But he can't open his mouth without that F word. Every second word is that F word. Makes you sick listening to him.

Are you going away this weekend? It's good to have someone to talk to. He says I'm feeling sorry for myself, looking for sympathy from everyone, and I'm lazy because I don't feel like cooking anymore. And he buys so much food. We have more food in the house now than when the six of us lived here. And no one to eat it. It's awful to waste food. Do you want some peaches? I can't talk to him anymore. He just has another rye. 'Stand up and be counted' is what he's always saying. What's that suppose to mean, I ask you? What's that go to do with me not feeling like cooking? He says mean things like you just don't know. Makes me feel like crying to think about the things he says. I'm sixty-one now. I'd like to quit working, but what am I going to do, staying at home seven days a week with him? Sometimes I think I'm ready for the old folks' place.

The other day he was mad because I came up the stairs too slow. He said I walk like an old woman. And he says, "Look at you, no make-up on. You look like hell." What am I suppose to do? Dance up the stairs? He's not very understanding. Says he's got problems, too. Well I know he has. I'll give him that. He's right, with his diabetes and the plaque in his head. He has to take pills so the plaque won't build up. He could have a stroke. I know he's got problems. So look how he's handling them. He thinks he knows more about everything than anyone else does. You should be in the car with him when he's driving, even when he's sober. Every driver on the road is doing something wrong and he sees it all. He should have been a professor at the university, he's so smart.

Well, I'll get home now. Come over for a few minutes later, if you feel like it. You'll get the cat in if he doesn't show up before I go to bed? That is if you're not busy. I'm so tired lately.

No get up and go anymore, just can't be bothered anymore. To tell you the truth, I've lost interest in everything, even myself. Look at me with my heavy sweater and here you are in shorts. Doesn't even feel like we're going to have a summer this year. It's so chilly.

Final Chapter

Barbara LaValley

GETTING ON THE BUS TO NORTH BAY AT HUNTSVILLE SEEMED ALMOST an afterthought, after having spent the better half of the previous day travelling north from Toronto. I asked the driver to let me off at the junction of Highways 11 and 518, near Elmsdale.

The Northern Lights Motel, just outside of town, claimed to have reasonable canoe rental rates. Barry Levy, the owner and manager (and tour guide to the citified), offered to take the canoe and I up the access road and into Tim Lake.

"It's a good hour, hour and a half, canoeing to the first portage," he said. "Lake's a bit choppy today, with the wind and all, best you wait till six o'clock or so, give her a chance to glass over." Still, he didn't complain as he helped me to lift the canoe out of the truck and down to the makeshift dock. We arranged a time, four days ahead, when he would meet me here for the ride back.

"You sure you don't need nothing? That little pack you got going to get you by?" he mumbled, and gave me a once-over from the corner of his eye.

"I'm an Indian," I smiled, "I eat roots."

"Oh well, that's different, though, ya know, you don't look like no Indian from around here. These women all got whatcha might call 'padding'. You know, more meat on them. 'Cept in the behind. Don't seem to round out down there. Well, I ought to get back to work. I'll be seeing you Wednesday then. Six o'clock." He turned, with a perfunctory wave, and strode off.

"Crazy mixed-up Indians," I heard him murmur, "seems funny, a woman up here all by herseif. No husband to look after her ... wouldn't catch my missus doing such a fool thing ... no sir!"

As he leaned out of the truck window, he said, "You make sure you don't leave no food laying around. Bears don't have no sense when they smell food. They'll tear you up! You tie it in a tree away from your tent and far out on the limb, and don't go too close to no female animals, they got young now." His tires spewed gravel at the turn, and he was gone.

Hauling my belongings into the canoe, I paused and placed a few fieldstones in the bow to keep it level in the water. The first few dips of the paddle were hesitant. Water's cold, I thought, cold and colder. I drifted with the water's flow and, quick as it was, managed not to spin around or mire myself in the reeds and lily pads.

Fall has always been my favourite time of the year. In the park, it was breathtaking. The trees were in full colour. Flowering grasses and shrubs competed for the light, their faces upturned and dancing in the breeze. Each small sound rang out as if it were demanding to be heard. Water lapping at the shoreline. Wind whispering secrets between branches. I listened, though I could not say I understood. A river otter broke the surface of the water and gliding slowly by, waited for me to pass.

I neared the entrance to the lake and was amazed at the expanse of blue and gray. The whitecaps alone told me that it would be a rough crossing. I could barely make out a portage marker in the distance. Though Levy had warned me and I knew I would be at risk, I decided to head directly across the lake.

The gusts of wind blew across the water, rippling its skin and receiving answering shivers through mine.

Heading into the curl, I rode the crests as they propelled the canoe towards perdition. A loon called from somewhere on the lake: distress or loneliness. It made little difference, I could answer both.

My attention wandering for a moment, I panicked as water came into the canoe. I became more and more afraid that it would overturn and I would lose my life there in this water where I did not belong. I paddled with all my strength, gasping for air, tearing my muscles at the bone until at last, the canoe shuddered and scraped onto the rocks near shore.

Absurd, how that foundation of rock and stone moulding to my foot gave me cause to laugh. The omnipotence of wind and water. What a fool it was. It could have had me, but I beat it. I won this time!

I dragged my belongings into a clearing, covered myself and slept. I dreamt of bears.

It was morning and I heard a scuffling noise in the brush. Opening one eye, I saw a grayjay hop onto the ground and study me, as if I might be edible.

Food. I hadn't any. Hadn't brought any. For that was to be the test after all. I would live or die in this place, on my own.

I'd brought matches for building a fire. And finding an old coffee can, I filled it with lake water and put it onto boil. Gathering cedar sprigs for tea took only a minute or two and I then sat down to think.

I thought about my dream about bears the night before. There had been one, who came to me from amongst a group of them. They'd been hiding in the bush, outside of my field of vision. The bear approached me walking upright, as if it were making a concession to my human stance, which was somehow beneath its four-pawed connection to the earth. Even now, I knew I could sense it watching me, awake and aware. It would come back and I knew I would wait for it.

My purpose here was to end my life. I had grown weary of my human form, my existence. I hoped that the stories and legends of my childhood were true: that I could become something other than what I was, and leave behind this overwhelming weight of "humanity."

It had not been a joyous thing to be "of the people," to be always searching for validation, love, and self-respect. To find, after years of denial and displaced purpose, that to be Indian, Native, was to be truly denied.

The relationship between the earth, its creatures and I was no longer distinct and understood, as it had been in generations past.

I could not longer acquiesce to being defined by the non-Native world. Nor by those of my own nation, people who knew not who they were or why they existed or by what right, other than that determined by their religious affiliations.

I had not decided what my death would be; I simply trusted that it would come. God, the Creator, would take pity on my inept embrace of mortality and release me.

As a youth I had run away from authority and the inevitable lockup environments. Screaming silent frustration into the world, I was peerless, or so I'd thought. Throughout the many disappointments and changes of being shuffled about, I maintained a desire to be loved, "saved" by someone, something. But no catalytic personality, nothing that wasn't trying to offer me entrance into street-life, prostitution and drugs, presented itself. There were plenty of those offers, but I avoided them. Luck? Maybe.

Later, when I was older and searching for myself through my tenuous connection with a long-absent mother, I began to search through my "traditional Native culture," only to find that the definition of that belief system continued to elude me. There was no cemented structure, like the Catholic school, nor was there the peace of agnosticism. It was, however, easier in its malleability.

I felt I could belong, and for a while, it was enough. After a few years, my ready beliefs were wearing thin. It seemed as though I was required to judge. It saddened and terrified me each time another "born-again pagan" like myself decried or denounced someone "of the people" for their infidelity, or poverty, or materialism, or drunkenness, or beauty, or ugliness, or education or cruelty or kindness, or degree of Native blood. They themselves had most of the former qualities but not enough of the blood. Not enough to make them acceptable to the self-proclaimed Native and non-Native "geneticists" whose degrees were as imagined as their empathy for the "rootless one," the mixed-breed, those of us without the oriental eye-fold or Mongolian spot at the small of our backs. While still they denied any bias or bigotry, I had lived it along with countless others.

Why did we do it? Was this what being human wrought? To be eternally held in judgment, to be found lacking simply because we were what we were, human, fallible? I wanted no more of it. I was dying inside, without choice and without purpose. Now I would choose.

Motherhood had not quieted my fears but instead allowed them to envelop another, smaller being. She waits, grown but still connected to me. She waits for me to telephone, to write, to drop by. I hope that she will forgive me and love me still.

A red squirrel chattered a warning. Or perhaps it was merely hungry. Do they feel the things we do? Do they worry themselves to death, towards death, like I have done?

Having had an inclination to observe animals growing up, I believed I understood them. Protective of their young like us humans, they are affectionate and resourceful, but above all, territorial and aggressive. In the world of people these things were not spoken of. Instead, our values are thought to be superior, full of intellectualization and controlled emotion. But are they, really?

I hadn't meant to think about food, but there it was. I dug up a few cattails and cooked them over the fire. They tasted like green corn.

It was hot in the sun, and I took shelter under a nearby canopy of trees. Cool green needles, long and clean-smelling.

The bush creatures happened along in a steady procession — a moose waded up the shoreline while a turkey vulture banked overhead, scanning the ground for carrion. They did not seem to fear my presence in the slightest, but acknowledged it within their continuing activities. I lay there awaiting drowsiness, but none came. A snake slithered through the grasses. It edged ever so slowly towards me, blinking its eyes, a vertical pupil dilating. Big and blackish-brown with geometric markings on its back: a rattlesnake? Would it strike? I could not move. I felt for the deerskin bag that held my medicines and offered it to the creature.

"Will you kill me?" I asked, hoping that it would rather than leave me to wait.

No answer. Foolish to ask a snake to speak? It came slightly closer and reared its head above the ground. I reached for the small sweetgrass braid around my wrist and threw it into the fire. As the smoke curled upwards I prayed that whatever was to be would happen quickly. Painlessly.

"Come! I will NOT wait. Take me now — OR GO! Do not play with me!" Daring the snake to act, I sat upright and threw up my hands, as though to harm it.

A twist of tail and it was gone. Perhaps the snake had only been a dream? No. It had been real enough. I leapt up to seek it out, to cause it to perform its obligatory function — Cleopatra knew. Gone; well then. I returned and put my back against the tree trunk. I would wait.

I squinted at the sun and, looking back down, found myself in another place.

I was no longer in the forest, leaning against the trunk of a white pine, but in a room with whitewashed walls and shabby furniture. There were children playing and teasing one another. Not mine, but in my care. After what seemed an eternity, I managed to argue and cajole them into lying down to rest. I realized then that I was again amongst "the people." Their parents were at ceremonies and, as I was unable to go because of my menses (supposed to be unclean), the children had been left with me for the day. All ten of them.

Exhausted, I moved to lie on the tattered couch, to sleep — to leave again? A door opened and a bright light washed in, shining upon my face and surrounding the shadow of a man. He walked into the room and as he did, I found myself looking him over for imperfections and finding none. No creases in his smooth white cotton shirt and pants, no dust clinging to his skin from the dirt yard out front, no beads of sweat on this hot day.

"Who are you? What do you want? I don't know you. DO I?" No sound, only a steady gaze as he felt behind himself for a place to lie down and found one where there had been none before.

I panicked, and feeling he would not explain, demanded that he leave. The children rose and ran to him, shielding him from me. No matter. He will leave. Why should he stay behind with me, here, as a watcher of children? He turned and, with a smile, directed them to rest and be still. They did, and I was amazed at the ease and comfort with which he controlled them.

He rose and walked away from me, silently willing me to follow. I did and found I could not bear to be in close proximity to him. I forced myself a step forward and a sharp pain flooded my body, halting me and pinning my feet to the floor.

"Come over here, by me," he said, his voice undulating. I found I could slide forward a step at a time. One, two and three, a few feet behind and to the left.

He moved aside as if to permit me to see what lay in front of him. "Do you see them? The fish. Do you see their colours?" I looked and saw he had somehow conjured up a glass aquarium full of tropical fish. Curious! I looked closer, mesmerized by the flashing colours.

"People are like these fish. Some small, some large, different shapes and colours. But THEY ARE ALL FISH and they came from the same place, all those millions of years ago." His back toward me, he continued, "Once, people were the same, the same ..." I was no longer behind this man, in a house, but flying through the air, drifting down through the clouds to view the earth.

As I neared the earth, I felt my body being directed by some gentle force towards a familiar location, which seemed to me to be reminiscent of the northeastern American continent. Tall, dark fir trees blanketed the landscape. The air felt thick and moist, fresh with that tree-smell that children wrinkle their noses at and adults remember. I hovered in the air. The buoyancy of the mist felt good on my belly and thighs.

Then, I saw them. The people. I could hear the man's voice in my ear as he explained to me, "The people, the first ones, were as you see them now, tall and firm bodied, devoid of illness, hunger and pain ..."

They seemed beautiful to me and though I was far above them, I could see their movements as if I were truly an eagle. I saw the smiles on their faces, the work in their hands, the caresses from mother to child and between lovers. I felt happy and content.

The sun filtered his words as they pressed their way into my consciousness: "When the Creator brought forth the People they were given many things, precious gifts of plants and animal life to sustain them, feed them, clothe them, warm their bodies. They were given the task of caretaking our planet and in doing so, were encouraged to use the gift of Choice, to make correct decisions, to bring kindness and just action to all that they would do."

I watched and saw the motions, the ritual libation, fluids poured onto the ground, the leaving of tobacco when gathering medicine, the burning of sweetgrass and sage. These made sense to me now, had meaning. I KNEW WHY these things were done without having to analyze or seek rationales. They were done to give thanks and to show appreciation for life.

Closing Prayer

Jacqui Lavalley

I BEGIN TO FEEL MY OWN HEALING WATER FLOW FREELY FROM MY EYES. Those "long time ago" memories are powerful experiences. I could hear my momma saying quietly, "Bizaahnnmah, wey wehna wey wehna dah biimosae."

Chi miigwech to all the women who shared with us a small part of their lives. Chi miigwech: Lee, Carol, Banakonda, Monica, Barbara, Dawn, Jane, Cat, June, Joy, Beth and Daria.

And to all those others who are inspired to share — may you receive the support and encouragement you require to continue in the "healing words."

Come home

Wai yaa hai
Wai yaa hai
Wai yaa hai

Biigiiyan Anishnaabe
Biigiiyan Anishnaabe
Biigiiyan Anishnaabe
Biigiiyan Anishnaabe
Biigiiyan Anishnaabe

The Women

The Writers

Cat Cayuga is Onondaga/Mohawk of the Six Nations Con-feder-acy. She is the mother of one child (to date). Cat works in various areas of the Arts and goes where the work needs to be done.

June Cayuga is Bearfoot Onondaga. She lives in Hamilton and works full-time as a cashier. The oldest of the writing workshop participants, "Grandma June" as she was called, reflects on that experience: "Thank you, N'nawah, for letting me join this sharing circle. I feel that, perhaps now, I may complete my own circle." This grandmother of three (to date), credits her daughter, Cat, with leading her back to the Native tradition.

Dawn Ireland-Noganosh grew up on the Oneida First Nations near London, Ontario. She is Bear Clan. She studied at Trent University, and received a Social Service Worker's Diploma from Loyalist College. After a short stint in administration with Native Earth Performing Arts, Dawn is now the publishing co-ordinator for INTO THE MOON project. Dawn is the mother of three children, and is a traditional dancer.

Lee Johns is of Ojibway-Odawattami descent and was born and raised in beautiful Neyaashiinigmiing, Saugeen Territory. She is Loon Clan and is one of nine children. She is extended-sister to 6 children, has 31 nieces and nephews (natural and extended), and she herself is the mother of one child, a daughter. She has returned to her Mediwiwin origin, and has a deep respect for all cultures and faiths. She loves learning about wellness of body, mind and spirit, and enjoys history, language, songs & dances, and original stories. Currently, she is working as a Community Development Support Worker.

Banankonda K.K.Bell is originally from the Rankin Reserve near Sault Ste. Marie, Ontario. She has an Honours B.A. in sociology from York University and an M.A. in psychology from the Adler Institute. She is an artist, and hopes to have an exhibition of her paintings in the near future. Her art merges with her other work as a therapist. Currently, she is teaching Native psychology and sociology at the First Nations Technical Institute. Banakonda has three children aged 21, 12 and 7.

Barbara LaValley is Wolf Clan from the Cornplanter (Allegheny) Reserve in Pennsylvania. She has four sisters and one brother — all budding writers. Barbara was involved with theatre during the 1980s. At that time, she was a fancy dancer and followed the Pow Wow trail. She also worked with A.N.D.P.V.A., beginning as a volunteer and working her way up to the position of assistant to the executive director. Currently, Barbara is in social services and works with Native groups and women's groups. She has a daughter aged 17, a son who is 2, and a new baby.

Carol Loft is Wolf Clan from the Tyendinaga Mohawk Territory. She is the oldest of nine children. For the past four years, she has been on a journey that involves healing childhood pain. "In this journey, I have grown and learned a great deal about myself. Beth Brant, as a facilitator of the writing workshop, was instrumental in what I wrote, at that time. She helped me find words that I didn't realized existed in me. For this I say Nia:wen!" Carol is married and has three beautiful children.

Monica McKay's Nisga`a name is Laax t'ok, and she is of the Killerwhale Clan of the Nisga`a Nation. She comes from the village of LaxK`alzap (Greenville, B.C.). She is currently living in Toronto and is working part-time at Ryerson Polytechnical University as the Aboriginal Students Co-ordinator. She is also working to complete a degree in social work. The writing workshops that Monica attended fulfilled a desire to explore and find support for her poetry. She also appreciated the leadership of Beth Brant. Monica would like to continue writing and would like to see other writing workshops happen.

Jane Peloquin is Micmac and was born in New Brunswick. She is a singer, songwriter and poet. She has travelled throughout Canada and lived for short periods in Calgary, Edmonton, Winnipeg, and Toronto. She is currently living and working in Thunder Bay. Between 1985 and 1988, Jane recorded two albums of original songs. She has also had work published in *Fireweed* Magazine.

The Facilitators

Beth Brant is a Bay of Quinte Mohawk from Tyendinaga in Ontario. She was born May 6th, 1941. She is the editor of *A Gathering of Spirit,* a ground-breaking collection of writings and artwork by Native women. (Firebrand Books, USA and Women's Press, Canada, 1988) She is also the author of *Food & Spirits,* a collection of essays (Women's Press, 1994). Her work has appeared in numerous Native, feminist and lesbian anthologies throughout North America. She is a mother and grandmother and lives with her partner of eighteen years, Denise Dorsz. Brant is currently working on a book of Tyendinaga Elders' oral history, *I'll Sing Til the Day I Die,* and a book of essays about Land and Spirit entitled *Testimony From the Faithful.*

Joy Asham-Fedoric is Cree. She is a writer and culture worker with a keen interest in desktop publishing.

Opening and Closing Prayer

Jacqui Lavalley is of the Ojibway Pottawatomi, Marten Clan of the Shawanga First Nation. She is Three Fires Society Midiwiwin Kwe first degree. She is a traditional Cultural Teacher at First Nations School in Toronto, and also counsels First Nations people who are just discovering themselves. She loves singing with First Nations women, also dancing and storytelling.

The Illustrator

Darla Fisher-Odjig is Ojibway-Pottawatomi from Wikwemikong First Nation on Manitoulin Island. She uses a wide range of media such as watercolours, charcoal, acrylic, inks and design pens. Her subjects are expressionistic and lean toward family unity. Darla is also a design artist-illustrator by profession.

The Editor

Lenore Keeshig-Tobias is an award-winning author, traditional Ojibway storyteller, and culture worker. She has five children and two grandchildren.